Straight Forward with Sci

LIGHT
AND
COLOUR

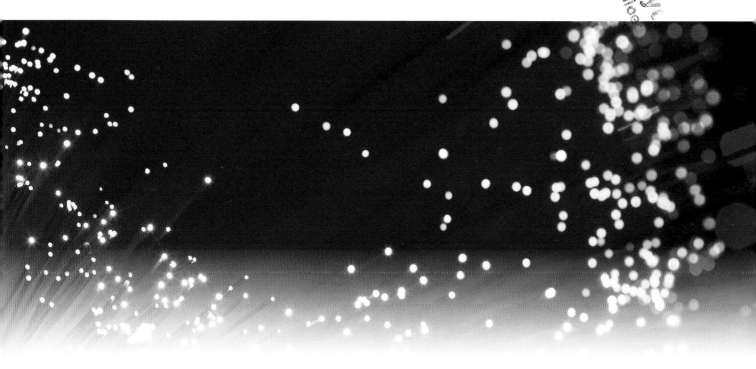

Peter Riley

W

To my granddaughter, Tabitha Grace.

Franklin Watts

Published in paperback in 2016 by the Watts Publishing Group
An imprint of Hachette Children's Group
Part of the Watts Publishing Group
Carmelite House
50 Victoria Embankment

An Hachette UK company
www. hachette.co.uk
www.franklinwatts.co.uk

ISBN: 978 1 4451 3549 6

Editor: Julia Bird
Designer: Mo Choy
Printed in China

Photo acknowledgements: Adrian_am13/Shutterstock: 9t. John A Anderson/Shutterstock: 28b. Andriano/
Shutterstock: 17. apiguide/Shutterstock: 28t, 31. Ase/Shutterstock: 21b. Roger Bamber/Alamy: 15r. Jeffrey
B Banke/Shutterstock: 20b. Bashutskyy/Shutterstock: 7br. Matthew Benoit/Shutterstock: 2, 27tl. Anthony
Berenyi/Shutterstock: 7bl. bikeriderlondon/Shutterstock: front cover. Blend Images/Shutterstock: 13t.
Brandon Bourdages/Shutterstock: 23t. Catolia/Shutterstock: 9b. Cobalt 88/Shutterstock: 26b. Colette3/
Shutterstock: 29t. dvoevnore/Shutterstock: 11tl. Elenamiv/Shutterstock: 11b. Juergen Faelchie/Shutterstock:
18r. Fireflyphoto/Dreamstime: 5t. Foto_Ruhrgebeit/Shutterstock: 26t. Kurt_G/Shutterstock: 21t. Steve
Heap/Dreamstime: 14. Pavel Hyukhin/Shutterstock: 5b. Image State/Impact/Alamy: 13b. Bogdan Ionescu/
Shutterstock: 25b. David Ionut/Dreamstime: 6t. Eric Isselee/Shutterstock: 20t. JeniFoto/Shutterstock: 3, 25t.
Lil Kar/Shutterstock: 24b. katatonia82/Shutterstock: 23b. Kavram/Shutterstock: 12. Krasowlt/Shutterstock:
4b. Audrey_Kuzmin/Shutterstock: 27r. G Milosz/Shutterstock: 4t. MNI/Shutterstock: 8b. Mopic/Shutterstock:
22. NASA: 7t. Alta Oosthuizen/Shutterstock: 29b. Pakhnyushcha/Shutterstock: 24t. Mauro Rodrigues/
Shutterstock: 10. Roman Sakhno/Shutterstock: 6b. John Sarth/Shutterstock: 15tl. Science Photos/Alamy:
27b. Stockshoppe/Shutterstock: 19c. Tagla/Shutterstock: 18l. Diana Tallun/Shutterstock: 8t. Tazzymoto/
Shutterstock: 11tr. Upper Cut Images/Alamy: 16. Rob Wilson/Shutterstock: 19b.

Franklin Watts is a division of Hachette Children's Books, an Hachette UK company.
www.hachette.co.uk

FSC
www.fsc.org
MIX
Paper from
responsible sources
FSC® C104740

Contents

Where light comes from

The Earth's most powerful natural source of light is the Sun. It provides our planet with vital energy – without it there would be no life on Earth. Other sources of light, such as electric lights, are made by people so that we can see at night and in places where the Sun's light does not reach.

▌Most of the light on Earth comes from the Sun. It helps plants to grow.

LUMINOUS AND NON-LUMINOUS OBJECTS

Objects that give out light are called luminous objects. The most distant luminous objects are stars, like our Sun. They are millions of kilometres away from the Earth.

Most objects, however, are non-luminous – they do not give out light. We can only see them because luminous objects shine on them, and they reflect enough light to enable us to see them. Some objects reflect so much light that they shine. The Moon reflects the light of the Sun onto the Earth at night.

▌The Moon is the brightest non-luminous object we can see in the sky.

NATURAL LIGHT SOURCES

While the powerful natural light of the Sun gives light and energy to the Earth, other smaller natural light sources are found on the Earth itself. Glow worms and fireflies glow with a yellow-green light. During storms, flashes of lightning brighten the dark skies for a moment. Even in the darkness of the deep ocean there are fish that give out light from spots on their bodies.

❚ Fireflies give off light from the end of their body to attract a mate.

ARTIFICIAL LIGHT SOURCES

When people first discovered how to make fire, they discovered how to light up the dark as well as how to keep warm. Today, inventions such as candles, torches, lamps and television or computer screens give out light, and make our lives easier and more enjoyable.

❚ A campfire allows us to see at night when the Sun's light does not reach us.

INVESTIGATE
Make a list of all the light sources around you. How many are natural and how many have been made by people?

Light and energy

Light travels from its source, such as the Sun, to the object it is lighting. It moves in a straight line and travels faster than anything else we know of. The energy in a light ray can be used to power many different things.

I Light energy is a form of energy that we can easily see.

SPEED OF LIGHT

Light travels at 300,000 kilometres per second. The Sun is so far away that, even at this speed, its light takes eight minutes to reach Earth. If you are reading this book in daylight, the light reaching you now actually left the Sun eight minutes ago.

Light from a lamp travels at the same speed, but because it only has to travel a tiny distance to reach you, it seems to light up where you are instantly.

I Light can only travel in straight lines. Can you see the straight edges to these sunbeams?

INVESTIGATE

See how light travels in straight lines by shining a torch through a comb.

I Huge solar panels power the International Space Station satellite.

LIGHT ENERGY

The energy in light can be changed into other forms of energy. Solar cells on a calculator or solar panels on a satellite, for example, change the light energy into electrical energy. Green plants trap light energy in their leaves and use it to make food in a process called photosynthesis.

I This calculator is powered by energy from the Sun. It has a solar-powered battery.

I Green plants use some of the energy in light to make food.

Light and materials

When a ray of light hits an object, the light passes through the object, is reflected or is soaked up (absorbed). What happens to the light depends on the type of material it strikes.

TRANSPARENT MATERIALS

Some materials, such as glass, clear plastic and water, let rays of light pass straight through them. These materials are called transparent. A small amount of the light striking such materials, however, is reflected. This is useful to us, since it shows us the position of the surface of the material.

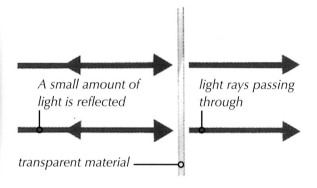

A small amount of light is reflected

light rays passing through

transparent material

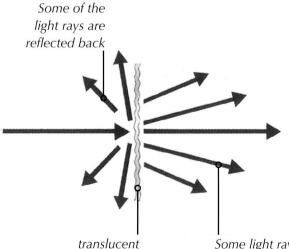

▌This jar is made from transparent glass so it is easy to see the sweets inside it.

TRANSLUCENT MATERIALS

A few materials, such as tissue paper, let light pass through them, but scatter its rays in all directions. These materials are called translucent. Some kinds of glass are made translucent by being given a rough surface.

▌We can only get an impression of the colours and shapes of the pens inside this translucent glass mug.

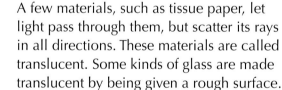

Some of the light rays are reflected back

translucent material

Some light rays scatter as they pass through

❙ The inside of this tunnel is in darkness because light cannot pass through the solid rock of the hill.

OPAQUE MATERIALS

Materials such as wood and brick do not let any light pass through them. They are called opaque materials. They soak up most of the light that reaches them. The small amount of light they reflect allows us to see them.

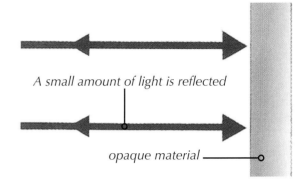

A small amount of light is reflected

opaque material

INVESTIGATE

Shine a torch on various objects around your home. Make a list of all the transparent, translucent and opaque objects you find. Were you surprised by any of your discoveries?

❙ This misty air scatters the Sun's light rays in many directions, making it difficult to see the landscape clearly.

Shadows

Light rays shining onto one side of an opaque object are absorbed or reflected. They cannot pass through the object and light up the area on the other side. A shadow forms behind the object.

I You can have fun with your shadow!

HOW SHADOWS ARE FORMED

The light rays that pass by the sides of the object keep moving in a straight line. They cannot bend round the side and fill the area behind the object with light. The dark area of the shadow may be slightly lit by rays reflected from other objects.

THE SIZE AND SHAPE OF A SHADOW

If an object is moved around in the light, different parts of it stop the light rays and the shape of the shadow changes.

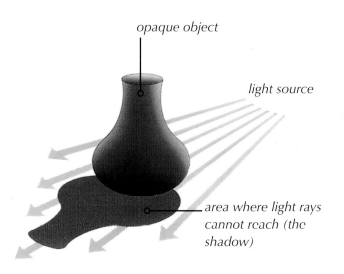

opaque object

light source

area where light rays cannot reach (the shadow)

HIGH AND LOW SOURCES OF LIGHT

At midday, when the Sun is high in the sky, shadows of people and buildings are very short. At the beginning or end of the day, though, when the Sun is low in the sky, the shadows are long.

▌The shadow of this tree is short because the Sun is high above it.

▌The shadow of this tree is long because the Sun is low down.

LIGHT FROM FAR AND NEAR

An opaque object blocks many of the light rays coming from the surface of a distant light source such as the Sun. This makes a shadow with a very clear edge.

An object cannot block so many of the light rays from the surface of a close light source, such as a lamp. This makes a dark shadow with a lighter edge. The dark part of the shadow is called the umbra and the lighter part is the penumbra.

INVESTIGATE

Place a pen on a table and shine a torch down on it. Raise the pen towards the torch and look for the umbra and penumbra. How far must you raise the pen to see them?

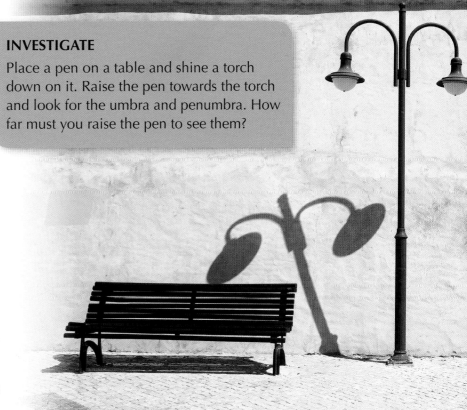

▌Some shadows, such as this bench and street lamp, have a sharp, clear edge.

Flat mirrors

When light strikes a mirror, most of the light is reflected from its smooth, shiny surface. This makes a picture in the mirror called an image.

HOW A MIRROR WORKS

The light rays in a beam of light travel in parallel lines. When they strike a smooth surface, they are reflected in the parallel lines. This arrangement of the light rays lets you see an image of where they came from in the surface of a flat mirror. Because the metal coating behind the mirror absorbs very little light, most of the rays are reflected. This makes the image bright and easy to see.

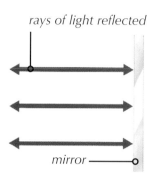

rays of light reflected

mirror

▌ Light rays are reflected by a flat mirror back along their paths.

NATURE'S MIRRORS

Other flat, shiny surfaces that reflect light well include water and polished metals. If you look into them, you may see a reflection of yourself in just the same way that you can see an image of yourself when you look into a mirror.

▌ Still water makes an excellent 'natural' mirror.

WRONG WAY ROUND

If you stand in front of a mirror, the light rays from your face strike the mirror head-on at 90° to the surface. The rays are reflected back along the path they came. The light from the right hand side of your face makes the left hand side of the face in your image. This means that the image in the mirror is reversed.

I Can you see how this girl's left hand becomes her right hand in the mirror's reflection?

I In a device called a periscope, light is reflected through two mirrors so a person can see over a wall or a crowd of people.

angle of incidence

angle of reflection

mirror

I For a flat mirror, the angle of reflection is the same as the angle of incidence.

REFLECTING A LIGHT BEAM

If a beam of light is shone from a torch onto a flat mirror at an angle, it is reflected from the mirror at the same angle. The angle at which the beam strikes the mirror's surface is called the angle of incidence. The angle at which the reflected ray leaves the surface is called the angle of reflection.

INVESTIGATE

Shine a torch through the teeth of a comb at a flat mirror. First shine the torch straight onto the mirror. Next change the angle at which the light shines on the mirror. What happens to the path of the reflected light?

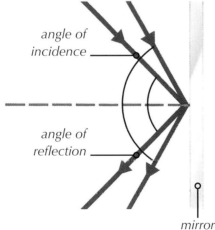

Curved mirrors

Some shiny surfaces are not flat. They still reflect light to make an image, but the images they make are not the same size as the object.

CONCAVE MIRRORS

When a shiny surface bends inwards, it makes a concave mirror. If you look in a concave mirror from a long way off, your image is small and upside down. If you move very close to the mirror, your image is magnified and the right way up. Concave mirrors can be used for shaving and to apply make-up. When a person puts their face close to the mirror, they see a magnified view of their skin.

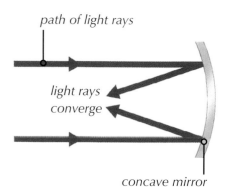

▌ Light rays hitting the surface of a concave mirror are reflected inwards.

▌This man is using a concave mirror to help him shave.

CONVEX MIRRORS

When a shiny surface bends outwards, it makes a convex mirror. When you look in a convex mirror from any distance, your image is always small, but it is always the right way up.

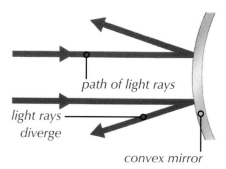

▌ Light rays hitting the surface of a convex mirror are reflected outwards.

I A convex mirror gives a wide view of the surroundings, and helps drivers to see around bends in the road.

I At some funfairs, concave and convex mirrors are put together to give you strange images.

INVESTIGATE

Use the inside of a spoon as a concave mirror and its outside as a convex mirror. What are the images like?

Bending light rays

Some light rays bend when they move from one transparent material to another. This bending is called refraction.

WHY LIGHT RAYS BEND

Light travels at different speeds in different transparent materials. When a light ray passes from one transparent material, such as air, to a second transparent material, such as glass, it changes speed.

If the light ray meets the surface of the second material head on at a right angle to it, the ray passes straight through and does not bend. If the light ray meets the surface between the materials at an angle, the change in speed makes the ray change direction and the light ray is bent.

STANDING IN WATER

If you stand in the water in a swimming pool and look down at your feet, your legs seem to be shorter than they really are. The light rays coming from your feet bend when they enter the air and look as if they come from another place near the surface. This makes your feet appear closer and your legs seem shorter.

▎The parts of these women which are underwater appear to be closer than they really are. This is because the light rays bend between the water and the air.

LENSES

A lens is a transparent piece of glass or plastic. It has opposite sides that are curved. A lens with two sides curved outwards is called a biconvex lens. A lens with two sides curved inwards is called a biconcave lens.

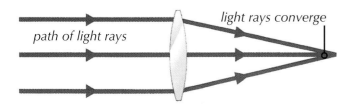

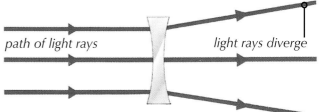

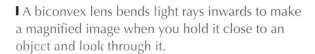

I A biconvex lens bends light rays inwards to make a magnified image when you hold it close to an object and look through it.

I A biconcave lens bends light rays outwards to make a smaller image when you hold it close to an object and look through it.

I A magnifying glass is made from a biconvex lens. Can you see how it enlarges the detail of these flowers?

INVESTIGATE

Fill a plastic bottle with water and shine rays of light through it from a torch and comb. Now squeeze the bottle. What happens to the light rays?

The eye

We are able to see things because light rays coming from them pass through the air and enter our eyes. There are many parts to the eye. They all help us to see.

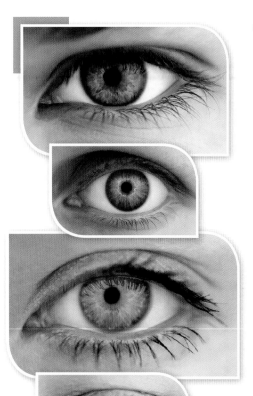

white of the eye

pupil

iris

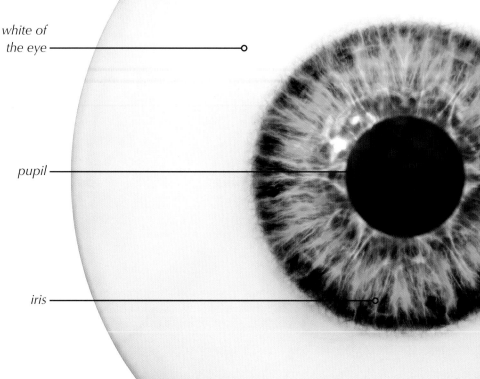

▮ The eyeball

OUTSIDE THE EYE

Most of the eyeball is covered in a white coat, but the front part of the eye is transparent. This part is called the cornea. Behind the cornea is a transparent liquid, and behind this is a coloured ring of muscles called the iris. The iris surrounds a black hole called the pupil. Light rays travel through the cornea and liquid, entering the eye through the pupil.

▮ An eye's iris can be brown, blue or shades of bluey-grey or green.

INSIDE THE EYE

Behind the pupil is a lens. It can change its shape and bend light rays so that they can make a picture inside the eye. After the light rays have passed through the lens, they move through a transparent jelly to the inside wall of the eye, or retina.

Here, the light rays form an upside down image of whatever the eye is looking at. The retina sends details of this image along nerves to the brain, which turns the image the right way up, allowing us to see.

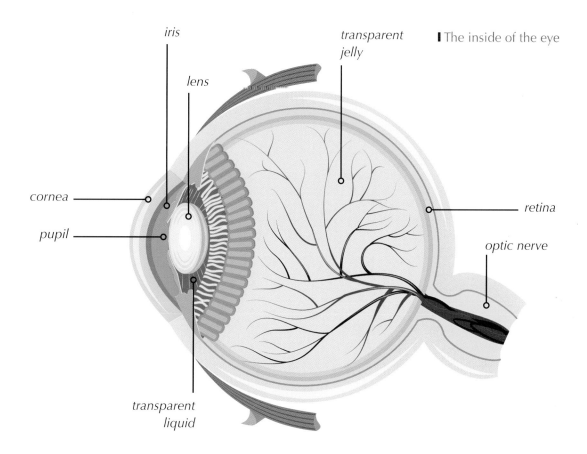

iris

transparent jelly

▌The inside of the eye

lens

cornea

pupil

retina

optic nerve

transparent liquid

▌Some people wear glasses to correct their eyesight.

GLASSES AND CONTACT LENSES

The lenses in some people's eyes bend the light rays too little or too much, making a blurred image on their retinas. Glasses or contact lenses bend the light in the opposite way to the lenses in these people's eyes so that they can see clearly.

INVESTIGATE
The eyelids blink to clean the front of the eye. How many times do you blink in a minute?

Animal eyes

Animals have different types of eyes depending on whether they are hunters who are looking for prey, or prey who have to watch out for attackers.

JUDGING DISTANCES

Each eye is able to see a certain area around it. This is called its field of view. If two eyes face in the same direction, like humans' eyes do, the fields of view overlap. This lets the animal judge distances well. Animals with eyes that face forwards are predators. They can judge the distance of their prey before they attack, helping them to catch the animal quickly.

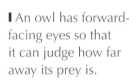

❙ An owl has forward-facing eyes so that it can judge how far away its prey is.

SEEING ALL AROUND

Animals such as deer and rabbits are prey for other animals. They have eyes that face in different directions. Each eye sticks out a little to give it a very wide field of view. If a rabbit had its eyes facing forwards, it would not be able to see its attackers creep up behind it.

❙ A deer's eyes are on opposite sides of its head to let it see all around, allowing it to look out for predators.

INSECT EYES

The top of an insect eye looks like a honeycomb. It is made up of lots of tiny eyes. Each tiny eye makes an image, which is linked to the images from the other eyes. The final image is made up in much the same way as a completed jigsaw puzzle.

I Flies have large numbers of small eyes to give them a wide field of view, making them difficult to swat away!

INVESTIGATE

Put a pen and its lid on a table. Close one eye and quickly pick them up and put the lid on the pen. How many goes does it take? Try again using both eyes.

I Because frogs spend so much of their time in the water, their eyes are on the top of their heads. Their bodies can stay safely underwater, while their eyes look out around them.

Colour in light

A ray of light from the Sun is made up of seven different colours visible to the naked eye. Together, these seven colours are known as a spectrum. It is these colours in light that give colour to everything around us.

SPLITTING UP THE COLOURS

If a ray of light strikes the side of a prism at an angle, it is bent or refracted as it goes into the glass. The ray travels through the prism until it strikes the other side where it is bent again as it passes into the air. The change in speed as the light goes through the prism and out again makes light separate into the seven colours of the spectrum – red, orange, yellow, green, blue, indigo and violet.

I Part of this beam of white light is reflected off the prism. The remaining part of the beam is split into a spectrum.

THE COLOURS OF AN OBJECT

When sunlight shines on something, some colours are absorbed and some are reflected. The reflected light gives the object its colour. A red object absorbs six colours, but reflects the red light. A green object absorbs six colours, but reflects the green light. A white object reflects all seven colours. A black object, on the other hand, absorbs all seven colours and so appears black.

A LIGHT FILTER

A light filter is made from a piece of transparent – but coloured – glass or plastic. It absorbs some of the colours of light but lets others pass through it. A red filter, for example, absorbs six colours and lets the red light pass through.

❚ The threads in these colourful clothes reflect a wide range of colours.

❚ Light filters can be used with stage lights to make special effects for concerts and shows.

Colours in the sky

The sky is sometimes full of wonderful colours. This is because the Earth's atmosphere can split light up into its various colours.

SKY COLOURS

The atmosphere is made up of a mixture of gases, water vapour and dust. Each gas is made up of particles called molecules. They scatter blue light in all directions and make the sky appear blue.

The Moon lights up the night sky.

NIGHT TIME

The night sky is dark when the part of the Earth below it has turned away from the Sun and is in shadow. The Moon beams down a strong, steady, reflected light to the ground. The weak light from distant stars is refracted by the air moving through the atmosphere, making them appear to twinkle.

INVESTIGATE

Put a few drops of milk in a transparent bowl full of water. Stir them up and shine a torch through the bowl. Look for the milk particles scattering the light, making the water appear slightly blue.

SUN COLOURS

The atmosphere splits up light from the Sun in the following way. For most of the day the Sun is high in the sky and the atmosphere lets yellow light in sunlight shine straight through. At dawn and dusk the Sun is lower and its light must shine through a thicker layer of atmosphere to reach us. This thicker layer scatters the yellow light but lets the red and orange through to give the colour to sunrise and sunset. (You must never look directly at the Sun as its light can damage your eyes.)

CLOUDS

Clouds are made from billions of tiny water droplets packed close together. Sunlight can shine through a cloud, but its light is scattered in all directions as it is reflected off the water droplets. This scattering of light makes clouds appear white. In a rain cloud there are so many raindrops that they absorb more light than they reflect, and so the cloud appears grey.

RAINBOW

When you watch rain falling, if the Sun is shining from behind you, you may see how the raindrops act as prisms and make a rainbow.

❙ Raindrops can split sunlight up into its seven different colours, creating wonderful rainbows.

Mixing colour

There are three colours of light and three colours of paint, which are each called the primary colours. The primary colours of light are red, green and blue. The primary colours of paint are yellow, cyan (blue) and magenta (bright pink).

MIXING COLOURED LIGHT

The three primary colours of light can be mixed to produce three secondary colours of light – yellow, magenta and cyan. If red and green light are mixed, yellow is made. Blue and red light together produce magenta and green and blue make cyan. When the three secondary colours are mixed they re-create the three primary colours – cyan and yellow make green, yellow and magenta make red and cyan and magenta make blue.

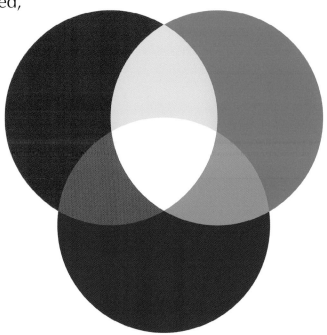

I Where all three primary colours of light overlap, white light is formed.

COLOUR TELEVISION

A television screen is made up of tiny dots called pixels. They produce colours when electricity passes through them. They work by combining just three colours – red, green and blue in a variety of ways to produce all the colours you see on the screen.

I The three primary colours make up most of the picture on this screen, but combining red and green light creates the yellow of the smaller flowers.

MIXING COLOURED PAINT

The colour in paint is made by small solid particles called pigments. They are spread out through the liquid part of the paint. Each pigment absorbs some colours in sunlight and reflects others. The three primary coloured pigments of yellow, cyan and magenta can be used to make many other different colours. For example, when yellow and cyan pigments are mixed together, they absorb all the colours from each other except green, so this is the colour of the paint they make.

❚ Paint samples are produced by paint manufacturers to show some of the many colours that can be made by mixing the primary colours of paint.

THE COLOURS IN INK

Some inks are made from mixtures of different coloured dyes. The dyes can be seen by placing a drop of ink on filter paper and putting drops of water on it.

INVESTIGATE

Put a spot of black ink on a piece of filter paper and dip it in water (right). What colours do you see as the ink spreads out?

❚ As the water mixes with the black ink on this piece of filter paper, the ink starts to separate into different colours.

Colours in animals

Some animals have amazingly colourful bodies. These colours serve useful purposes, helping them to hide, to find a mate or to warn other animals of their presence.

I A peacock displays his colourful feathers in order to attract a partner.

COLOURS FOR DISPLAY

The males of some kinds of animals are brightly coloured in order to attract a mate for breeding. The male guppy fish, for example, displays his bright colours by swimming in front of the female. In the same way, the males of many kinds of birds are extravagantly coloured. They use their colours, their songs and their movements to attract a mate.

COLOURS FOR WARNING

Some animals are poisonous if they are eaten. They have bright colours to warn off predators. Many caterpillars are safe from insect-eating animals because the animals recognise their colourful warning signals. A young animal may attack a poisonous caterpillar, but spits it out when it tastes the poison. The animal quickly learns not to try to feed on that type of caterpillar again.

I The bright colours of a monarch butterfly caterpillar warn predators that it is poisonous.

HIDING AWAY

Many animals use colours to camouflage their bodies and hide from predators. Their bodies may be just one colour, for example the brown coat of a deer helps the animal hide in the trees of a wood or forest. Other animals, such as some frogs, use blotches of different colours to help break up the outline of their bodies. This makes them more difficult to see.

❙ A leopard's spotty coat makes it difficult to see in its grassland habitat. This allows it to sneak up on its unsuspecting prey!

INVESTIGATE

Look at an area of grass, soil and stones and make a drawing of a local animal. Paint the animal in colours that would camouflage it in the area you have chosen.

❙ Special pigments in a chameleon's skin allow it to swiftly change colour.

COLOUR CODE

Some animals, such as chameleons, can even change the colour of their skin. They do this to control their body temperature. A cold chameleon may go dark to absorb more heat, for example, while a hot one may turn pale to reflect heat away. They also use colour to communicate with other chameleons – becoming dark when angry and colourful when they are ready to mate.

Glossary

angle of incidence – the angle at which a light ray strikes a mirror.

angle of reflection – the angle at which a light ray is reflected away from the surface of a mirror.

atmosphere – the layer of gases that we call the air and which covers the surface of the Earth.

biconcave lens – a lens with two surfaces curved inwards.

biconvex lens – a lens with two surfaces curved outwards.

caterpillar – a stage in the life cycle of butterflies and moths.

concave mirror – a mirror that has a surface that curves inwards.

converge – when light rays coming from different directions meet at the same point.

convex mirror – a mirror that has a surface that curves outwards.

cornea – the transparent front part of the eye.

diverge – when light rays separate and go in different directions.

firefly – an insect which gives off light from its abdomen.

image – a picture seen in a mirror or made by a lens focusing light.

insect – an animal with six legs and usually two pairs of wings.

iris – the coloured part of the eye.

International Space Station – a space station in orbit above the Earth on which astronauts live and carry out experiments.

lens – a piece of transparent material used to alter the path of rays of light passing though it.

light filter – a piece of coloured glass or plastic that lets light of one colour pass through it.

luminous object – an object that gives out light, for example the Sun or an electric light bulb.

magnified image – an image that appears larger than the object from which it is made.

molecules – groups of particles called atoms that make up most materials in the universe.

non-luminous object – an object that does not give out light. It is seen because of the light that it reflects from its surface.

opaque material – a material through which light cannot pass.

parallel lines – lines that lie next to each other and which are the same distance from each other all the way along their length.

penumbra – the light grey edge to a shadow.

periscope – a device in which light is reflected by mirrors so a person can see around a corner or over a high wall.

pigment – a material that gives colour.

pixel – the smallest part of a picture generated on a TV or computer screen.

predator – an animal that feeds on other animals.

prey – an animal that is eaten by other animals.

prism – a block of glass with a triangular shape.

pupil – the black hole at the centre of the iris in the eye.

rainbow – the spectrum produced in the sky when light shines through raindrops.

reflection – a picture of a scene or object seen on a smooth surface such as a mirror or on calm water.

refraction – a process in which the path of a ray of light is changed as it passes through a transparent material.

retina – the part of the eye that is sensitive to light.

satellite – a machine that moves around the Earth in space.

shadow – the dark area behind an object where rays from a light source cannot reach.

solar cell – a device that changes some of the energy shining on to it into electrical energy, and which then makes a current of electricity.

solar panel – a structure made up of a number of solar cells.

spectrum – a band of seven colours that make up white light. The colours are red, orange, yellow, green, blue, indigo and violet.

translucent material – a material through which some light passes but does not allow objects on the other side to be clearly seen.

transparent material – a material through which light passes and that allows objects on the other side to be clearly seen.

umbra – the darkest part of a shadow that lies inside the lighter penumbra.

Index

ABOUT THIS BOOK

This aim of this book is to provide information and enrichment for the topic of light in the Upper Key Stage 2 UK Science Curriculum. There are five lines of scientific enquiry. By reading the book the children are making one of them – research using secondary sources. The text is supported by simple investigations the reader can make to experience what has been described. Many of these investigations are simply illustrative to reinforce what has been read and practise observational skills, but the following investigations are also examples of types of scientific enquiry. Grouping and classifying: pages 5, 9; Pattern seeking: page 13; Observations over time: pages 19, 27; Comparative test: pages 21, 29.